Experience the

Passion

of Christ

A devotional based on the Stations of the Cross

Marty Schoenleber, Jr.

The Sojourning Press / **Bolingbrook, IL**

Experiencing the Passion of the Christ
Published by *The Sojourning Press,* 2005

ISBN: 0-9766853-0-2

Printed in the United States of America

Contents

Foreword

Faith feeds on Jesus Christ. The Savior who gives spiritual life will nourish that life as you draw near to Him in worship.

Experience the Passion of Christ will feed your soul as you ponder the journey of Jesus to the cross. These fourteen meditations will help you to enter into the sufferings of Jesus and will show you how His death and resurrection can touch and change your life today.

Marty Schoenleber tells the story of the passion as it happened. Then He offers a short and insightful reflection on each part of the story and turns the truth into prayers that will help you to respond back to God.

I am delighted to commend this excellent book to you. May God use it to nourish your soul and strengthen your faith as you draw near to Jesus Christ.

Colin S. Smith
Senior Pastor
Arlington Heights Evangelical Free Church
Arlington Heights, IL

Acknowledgements

How would pastors get anything done without the faithful servants of Christ in their care? Special thanks to Lorinda Carbonara for her editing of the text and to Carol Gundersen for her illustrations and partnership in the interactive ***Experiencing the Passion of Christ*** held at New Song Church.

Thanks to Betty Hamm for her cover design and to Pastor Bob Ooms for his artistic eye and photo for the front cover. To all of you, named and unnamed who made this project possible in the midst of transition and deadlines, thank you. Your love for Christ and encouragement has been invaluable.

Thanks too to Colin Smith for his gracious consent to write the Foreword. May God give the body of Christ many more servants like you.

Finally, I want to thank my wife, Stephnie, for her love and confidence through twenty years of marriage. "Many have done excellently, but you have exceeded them all."

For any errors of judgment or sensitivity, I take full responsibility and apologize to the reader in advance. Please forgive me.

Preface

Awe. That is what I felt as a young Catholic boy coming into the church of my youth. The smell of decades of incense, the raised alter where the priest spoke his strange Latin words, the pictures of Christ's passion that surrounded the worshipers—all of this combined to produce *awe* in my spirit.

Each element drew me, but it was the pictures of Christ's passion that were the most moving. I would sit in the pew, my mind often distracted from whatever was happening in the service, and my eye would wander to those images from the last hours of the Savior's life and *awe* would flood my soul.

They told me that Jesus loved me and I couldn't get over that marvelous fact. It both inspired and terrified me. I saw what He sacrificed for me and knew that such agony endured, could only be the result of love. It was both incomprehensible and wonderful. Jesus—God, loved me.

Those images hanging on the wall were part of an ancient tradition called, *The Stations of the Cross.* All through my childhood, those images and the captions summarizing the Gospel accounts of those painful hours in the life of Christ were used by the Spirit of God to call my heart toward Himself. They wooed me, along with bits and pieces of the gospel narrative, to the "perfect love that casts out fear" (1 John 4:18). They also convicted me that I needed a Savior—I needed Jesus to rescue me from my sin because it was my sin that caused Him to endure such treatment "at the hand of sinners" (Matthew 26:45).

It wasn't until my freshman year of college that God in His sovereign mercy and grace, wrestled my spirit to the ground and drew me to Himself in repentance and adoration. Thirty-one years have passed. My repentance sometimes wanes. My adoration and service for my King has never been complete. I am a struggling saint as are all the reclamation projects He calls His followers.

In my struggle to serve Him and love Him better today than yesterday, I mine the Scripture, I seek accountability and instruction from my brothers and sisters in Christ, and I seek the counsel and example of those who have left a mark of faithfulness in the history of the church.

This little book is part of the harvested fruit of that struggle. It is a meditation on the texts in the Gospels that tell us of the last hours of our Savior's stunning expression of love for us. It follows the general path of the ancient Roman Catholic tradition of the Stations of the Cross. But, as a Protestant centered in the text of Scripture for my devotion to Christ, I have substituted five new meditations to replace those elements that are more traditional than scriptural in nature.

My hope is that these pages will help all who read them to worship the Savior "in spirit and truth" (John 4:23-24). My prayer is that your love and appreciation for the One "who demonstrated His love" in dying for us (Romans 5:8) will deepen in both its passion and expression.

One Final Note: It is always a challenge in a book of devotion and worship to help the reader enter into the subject with a proper sense of awe and reverence. One of the lengthiest discussions that the editorial board had in this regard was what to do with the pronouns referring to Christ and deity. How do we help the reader? Do we accommodate modern trends away from the capitalization of pronouns in reference to deity or do we go back to the traditional pattern?

In the end it was decided that the audience for whom this book was written would value the traditional pattern more than the modern. I have made one exception. Where the speaker is a clear antagonist and non-believer in Christ (for example Pilate, or the Pharisees) I have retained the lower case for the pronouns referring to Christ. My hope is that this will heighten the sense of drama and be an aid to the reader's devotion.

> To God be the glory.
> Marty Schoenleber, Jr.
> Ash Wednesday
> February 9, 2005

Chapter 1

The Savior sweats drops of blood in the garden.

Adapted from the accounts of
Matthew 26:36-46, Mark 14:32-42, Luke 22:39-46

He asks for the cup to pass.

Then Jesus went with them to a place called Gethsemane, and He said to his disciples,

"Sit here, while I go over there and pray."

A short time later, He said to them,

"My soul is very sorrowful, even to death; remain here, and watch with Me."

And taking with Him Peter and the two sons of Zebedee (James and John), He began to be sorrowful and troubled.

"Pray that you may not enter into temptation."

And He withdrew from them about a stone's throw, knelt down, and fell on His face to pray.

"My Father, if it be possible, let this cup pass from Me; nevertheless, not as I will, but as You will."

And He came to the disciples and found them sleeping.

So He said to Peter,

"Could you not watch with Me one hour? Watch and pray that you may not enter into temptation. The spirit indeed is willing, but the flesh is weak."

Again, for the second time, He went away and prayed,

"My Father, if this cannot pass unless I drink it, Your will be done."

And again He came and found them sleeping, for their eyes were heavy with sorrow, and they did not know what to answer Him.

So, leaving them again, He went away and prayed for the third time, saying the same words. And there appeared to Him an angel from heaven, strengthening Him. And being in agony, He prayed more earnestly; and His sweat became like great drops of blood falling to the ground. Then He came to the disciples and said to them,

"Are you still sleeping and taking your rest? Sleep and take your rest later on. See, the hour is at hand, and the Son of Man is betrayed into the hands of sinners. Rise, let us be going; see, My betrayer is at hand."

Devotional

A lonely place filled with shadows overlooking the City of David, the place from which Jesus had sent two of His disciples to prepare the room for the Passover celebration—that is the place of His agony in the garden.

Here He asks His disciples to pray—but they did not pray.

Here He prays for the cup to pass—but it did not pass.

And here He asks that the will of the Father be done—and the will of the Father was done.

For Isaiah wrote (Isaiah 53:10a):

> BUT THE LORD WAS PLEASED TO CRUSH HIM,
> PUTTING HIM TO GRIEF;

That night He was crushed for you.

While His disciples slept, His betrayer came.

You won't sweat blood as you meditate on the suffering of Christ on your behalf. But you can try to imagine the anguish of Christ as He contemplated laying His life down for you in the mystery of His sacrifice for us all.

Lord Jesus,

my heart runs away from suffering

like water down a hill.

I shrink back from suffering

at nearly every chance.

But You willingly took upon Yourself my sin.

Your love for me is amazing and my spirit is

bowed in awe of Your matchless sacrifice.

Thank You for the wonder of Your love.

Thank You for laying down Your life for me.

Help me to live the whole of my life for You.

In Your steadfast name, I pray.

Amen.

Chapter 2
The Savior is betrayed with the kiss of a friend.

Adapted from the accounts of
Mt 26:47-56; Mk 14:43-50; Lk 22:47-53, Jn 18:4-11

The friend / betrayer comes.

While He was still speaking, Judas, the betrayer and one of the twelve, came leading a great crowd wielding swords and clubs along with the chief priests and the elders of the people. Then Jesus, knowing all that would happen to Him, came forward and said to them,

"Whom do you seek?"

"Jesus of Nazareth," they said.

"I am He."

Upon hearing this they drew back and fell to the ground. So He asked them again,

"Whom do you seek?"

"Jesus of Nazareth," they said again.

"I told you that I am He. So, if you seek Me, let these men go."

This was to fulfill the word that He had spoken: *"Of those whom You gave Me I have lost not one."* (See Psalm 109:8, Acts 1:16-20, John 13:18, and Psalm 55.)

Now the betrayer had given them a sign, saying, "The one I will kiss is the man; seize him and take him away under guard."

Jesus said to him,

"Friend, do what you came to do."

And he came up to Jesus at once and said, "Greetings, Rabbi!"

and Judas drew near to Jesus to kiss Him and Jesus said,

"Judas, would you betray the Son of Man with a kiss?"

Then they came up and laid hands on Jesus and seized Him. And when those who were around Him saw what would follow, they said,

"Lord, shall we strike with the sword?"

And behold, Simon Peter, one of those with Jesus, drew his sword and struck Malchus, the servant of the high priest, and cut off his ear.

Then Jesus said to him,

"Put your sword back into its place. For all who take the sword will perish by the sword. No more of this! Shall I not drink the cup that the Father has given Me? Do you think that I cannot appeal to My Father, and He will at once send Me more than twelve legions of angels? But how then should the Scriptures be fulfilled, that it must be so?"

And He touched the servant's ear and healed him.

Devotional

How devastating to be betrayed by the kiss of a long-time friend.

Three years Judas had lived at His side. Three years he had heard the Master teach, watched Him pray, experienced His power over sickness and life and death. He was there when the Master healed the lepers, walked on water, gave sight to the blind, and raised a little girl from the dead.

Judas had held one of the twelve baskets of leftovers after the feeding of the 5000.

Psalm 55 captures the agony of such a betrayal.

> HIS SPEECH WAS SMOOTHER THAN BUTTER,
> BUT HIS HEART WAS WAR;
> HIS WORDS WERE SOFTER THAN OIL,
> YET THEY WERE DRAWN SWORDS. (V. 11)

Probe your own heart. You know what it is like to be betrayed. Remember the sorrow,
> the disappointment,
> the depression,
> the darkness?

Imagine those feelings being multiplied by the millions who have claimed the name "Christian" and who have betrayed the perfection of His sacrifice with less than passionate lives.

But don't stop there. Remember that you too have betrayed others. Remember that, as God, He knew every one of your yet-future betrayals and still He laid His life down for you.

Remember, and weep with delight at the cup from which He drank that night on the Mount of Olives in the garden of Gethsemane.

Betrayed but unbetraying Lord,

how majestic is Your holiness and love.

Thank You for calling me into

the family of God.

Help me to kiss like the grateful woman who

washed and kissed Your feet.

Keep me from a life that looks like the loyal

kiss of a friend and yet

betrays the magnificence of Your passion

for me.

In Your faithful name I pray.

Amen.

Chapter 3

The Savior is abandoned by the disciples and denied by Peter.

Adapted from the accounts of
Mt 26:55-56, 69-75; Mk 14:66-72;Lk 22:54-62

Abandoned and denied.

At that hour Jesus said to the crowds,

"Have you come out as against a robber, with swords and clubs to capture Me? Day after day I sat in the temple teaching, and you did not seize Me. But all this has taken place that the Scriptures of the prophets might be fulfilled. This is your hour, and the power of darkness."

Then all the disciples left Him and fled.

They seized Him and led Him away, bringing Him into the high priest's house, and Peter followed at a distance.

Now Peter was sitting outside in the courtyard below, and the crowd had kindled a fire in the middle of the courtyard where Peter was sitting. A servant girl of the high priest, seeing him warming himself, came up and said,

"You also were with Jesus the Galilean."

But he denied it before them all, saying,

"I neither know nor understand what you mean."

And when he went out to the entrance, another servant girl saw him, and she said to the bystanders,

"This man was with Jesus of Nazareth. He is one of them."

And again he denied it with an oath:

"I do not know the man."

After a little while the bystanders came up and said to Peter,

"Certainly you too are one of them, for your Galilean accent betrays you."

Then he began to invoke a curse on himself and to swear,

"I do not know the man."

And immediately, while he was still speaking, the rooster crowed.

And the Lord turned and looked at Peter, and Peter remembered the saying of Jesus,

"Before the rooster crows twice, you will deny Me three times."

And he went out and wept bitterly.

Devotional

Ancient courtyards could be dark and dangerous places. Anxiety and fear traveled together in the courtyards of power of the Roman Empire.

Less than twelve hours before, Peter declared that even if all abandoned Jesus, he would remain, though it cost him his own life. But Jesus had unmasked Peter's bravado.

"Before the rooster crows, you will deny Me three times." (John 13:38)

Three times, Peter was linked to Jesus.

Three times he denied knowing Him.

He denied knowing the One who in those very moments was walking toward the cross upon which Peter's sins would be atoned—yours too.

The third time was the worst. Peter was in the courtyard outside where Jesus was being tried. For a third time he denied knowing Jesus and then Jesus, from inside the high priest's house, looked at Peter. Can you imagine Peter's despair? He had proclaimed that he would die before he turned his back on the Master. Now the Master is looking at him after his third denial.

Peter remembered the Lord's words.

"And he went out and wept bitterly."

You weren't there. You don't know what you would have done under similar circumstances. But you have been in places that weren't dark or dangerous and still you denied the Savior. Maybe it was a grocery store, or a classroom, or a school yard, or a restaurant, or your son's ballgame. Somebody defamed the name of Christ, and you said nothing to claim Him as your own.

Lord Jesus,

it is so easy for me to point the finger

at Peter or anyone else,

but I have failed You in so many ways myself.

Thank You for knowing all my sin

and loving me anyway.

Help me to walk into and out of the alleys of life

and away from the fear of men.

Help me to live for an audience of One

all the days of my life.

In Your name I ask this.

Amen.

Chapter 4

The Savior is condemned to death by Pilate.

Adapted from the accounts of
Mt 27:21-26; Mk 15:9-15; Lk 23:18-25;Jn 18:33-40

Jesus is interviewed by Pilate.

So Pilate entered his headquarters again and called Jesus and said, "Are you the King of the Jews?"

"Do you say this of your own accord, or did others say it to you about Me?"

"Am I a Jew? Your own nation and the chief priests have delivered you over to me. What have you done?"

"My kingdom is not of this world. If My kingdom were of this world, My servants would have been fighting, that I might not be delivered over to the Jews. But My kingdom is not from the world."

Then Pilate said to him, "So you are a king?"

"You say that I am a king. For this purpose I was born and for this purpose I have come into the world—to bear witness to the truth. Everyone who is of the truth listens to My voice."

Pilate said to him, "What is truth?"

After he had said this, he went back outside to the Jews and told them,

"I find no guilt in him. But you have a custom that I should release one man for you at the Passover."

The governor again said to them,

"Which of the two do you want me to release for you? Do you want me to release for you the King of the Jews?"

For he perceived that it was out of envy that the chief priests had delivered him up. But the chief priests stirred up the crowd to have him release Barabbas instead. So they said,

"Barabbas."

Pilate said to them,

"Then what shall I do with Jesus who is called Christ?"

They all said, **"Let him be crucified!"**

Pilate addressed them once more, desiring to release Jesus, but they kept shouting,

"Crucify, crucify him!"

And he said a third time,

"Why, what evil has he done? I have found in him no guilt deserving death. I will therefore punish and release him."

But they shouted all the more,

"Crucify him!"

So when Pilate saw that he was gaining nothing, but rather that a riot was beginning, and wishing to satisfy the crowd, he took water and washed his hands before the crowd, saying,

"I am innocent of this man's blood; see to it yourselves."

And all the people answered,

"His blood be on us and on our children!"

Then he released for them Barabbas, and having scourged Jesus, delivered Him over according to their will to be crucified. Now Barabbas was a robber and a man who had been thrown into prison for an insurrection started in the city and for murder.

Devotional

Has any washbasin ever been as misused as the one Pilate used that day?

There he was. He sat in the seat of power. The opportunity was his. He could have dispensed justice. But he refused. He could see nothing to gain for himself, and so he declared himself innocent of the blood of Christ and moved on with the rest of his life.

Futile.

How could Pilate think that he could wash his hands of the blood of Christ?

Pilate wasn't innocent. Neither are we.

We are all guilty of the blood of Christ. Apart from the sacrifice He made, we all stand condemned. We were "dead in our transgressions and sins." (Ephesians 2:1, 5)

That's why we need a Savior.

That's why Jesus came.

Sinless Savior,

thank You for the exchange of Your life for my sin.

I deserved condemnation,

but instead You were condemned in my place.

Help me to live for the justice that You were denied.

Help me to respond to any injustice done to me

in ways that bring glory and honor to You.

Help me to stand against injustice

done to others who are made

in the image and likeness of You,

my God.

For Your glory, I ask this.

Amen.

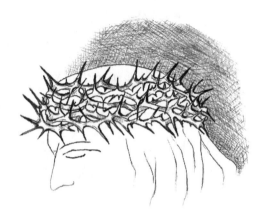

Chapter 5

The Savior is crowned with thorns.

Adapted from the accounts of
Mt 27:27-31; Mk 15:16-20; Jn 19:1-7

Jesus is flogged and crowned.

The soldiers of the governor took Jesus into the governor's headquarters inside the palace, and they gathered the whole battalion before Him. And they stripped Him and put a scarlet robe on Him, and twisting together a crown of thorns, they put it on His head and put a reed in His right hand. And kneeling before Him, they saluted and mocked Him, saying,

"Hail, King of the Jews!"

Pilate went out again and said to them,

"See, I am bringing him out to you that you may know that I find no guilt in him."

So Jesus came out, wearing the crown of thorns and the purple robe. Pilate said to them,

"Behold the man!"

And they spit on Him and took the reed and struck Him on the head. And when they had mocked Him, they took the purple robe and put His own clothes on Him and led Him away to crucify Him.

When the chief priests and the officers saw Him, they cried out,

"Crucify him, crucify him!"

Pilate said to them,

"Take him yourselves and crucify him, for I find no guilt in him."

The Jews answered him,

"We have a law, and according to that law he ought to die because he has made himself the Son of God."

Devotional

God incarnate.

The God of Abraham, Isaac and Jacob, the God of Moses, Joshua and Samson, the God of Samuel, David and Solomon, the God of Esther, Hezekiah and Nehemiah, the God of Isaiah, Jeremiah and Ezekiel stands before a mob bent on crucifying Him. With a word, He could destroy their power and disintegrate their bodies.

But He does not.

Instead, He allows them to beat Him, to flog Him, to mock Him, to crown Him with brutal scalp-piercing thorns.

The Psalmist captures the atmosphere: (PS 22:6-7)

> BUT I AM A WORM AND NOT A MAN,
> SCORNED BY MANKIND
> AND DESPISED BY THE PEOPLE
> ALL WHO SEE ME MOCK ME;
> THEY MAKE MOUTHS AT ME;
> THEY WAG THEIR HEADS;

Allow your heart to marvel at the restraint your Lord showed. He who possessed all power allows all the injustice of the moment to fall on Him.

Why?

Because, He came to give His life "a ransom for many" (Matthew 20:28).

Because He came to demonstrate His love, in that while we were yet sinners, He—the anointed fulfillment of Scripture, the Savior of the world—laid His life down for us (Roman 5:8),

You are one of the many, if you believe on His name. Is that not news worthy of both tears and rejoicing?

Ransomed Sacrifice for my sin,

thank You for the meekness

of Your stand that day.

You kept power under control so that I could be

ransomed from the death I deserved.

Help me to live in such a way that others never

view Your life as a museum exhibition,

but rather as a love letter written

in the blood of Your sacrifice.

In Your matchless name,

Amen.

Chapter 6

The Savior begins to carry His cross.

Adapted from the account of
Mt 27:32; Mk 15:21 Lk 23:26; Jn 19:17-18

Jesus shoulders the burden of the cross.

… and He went out, …

… bearing His own cross, …

… to the place called 'the place of the skull,' which in Aramaic is called Golgotha. Two others, who were criminals, were led away to be put to death with Him, one on either side, and Jesus between them.

As they went out, they found a man, a passerby coming in from the country, Simon of Cyrene by name, the father of Alexander and Rufus.

They seized Him and laid on Him the cross to carry it behind Jesus.

Devotional

Mel Gibson's movie *The Passion of the Christ* is a visually and emotionally assaulting film. It throws reality at us in a sensory barrage of images that lingers in the soul long after the movie ends. It is powerful. It is filled with devotion and has made box office history.

But it is not completely accurate or true to the biblical and historical record at all points. Jesus did not carry His cross.

He started to carry the cross but was too weak from the beatings He had received. So the cross beam upon which His sinless hands were nailed was laid upon the shoulders of Simon of Cyrene who walked behind Jesus.

Some might use this minor historical inaccuracy in the film to downplay the agony of Christ. "See," they might say, "It wasn't as bad as Mel Gibson made it look"

They would be wrong.

It was worse—far worse.

The torture of the cross He bore was not merely physical but spiritual and emotional. He was bearing the weight of the sins of all those who would believe in Him. No human being could help the Savior with that weight, but every human being who ever lived is in debt to the weight He bore that day.

Wonderful Savior,

glorious Lord, Immanuel, God-with-us,

thank You for bearing the burden

of my sin. It was my sin

that made Your burden so great.

Help me to know how much I have been forgiven

so that I will love much (Luke 7:47)

because

"Love so amazing so divine

demands my soul, my life, my all!"

Help me to give my all.

In Jesus' name,

Amen.

Chapter 7

Jesus meets the women of Jerusalem.

Adapted from the account of
Luke 23:27-32

The women of Jerusalem mourn.

And there followed Him a great multitude of the people and of women who were mourning and lamenting for Him. But turning to them Jesus said,

"Daughters of Jerusalem, do not weep for Me, but weep for yourselves and for your children. For behold, the days are coming when they will say,

'BLESSED ARE THE BARREN AND THE WOMBS THAT NEVER BORE AND THE BREASTS THAT NEVER NURSED!'

THEN THEY WILL BEGIN TO SAY TO THE MOUNTAINS,

'FALL ON US,'

AND TO THE HILLS,

'COVER US.'

FOR IF THEY DO THESE THINGS WHEN THE WOOD IS GREEN, WHAT WILL HAPPEN WHEN IT IS DRY?"

Devotional

Jesus—beaten and bruised and bloody beyond recognition—walks toward His destiny. Simon the Cyrene is next, carrying the cross that will lift Him up to His death. Following behind, multitudes of people are shouting, and the women of Jerusalem are mourning that no one is showing mercy to the merciful One.

And then Jesus turns around.

Perhaps Simon is taking a break. Perhaps he walks on past Jesus, and now the Savior is in the rear of the procession, face to face with the mourners.

He who is in distress and discomfort, "a dead man walking," turns and warns the daughters of Jerusalem. Even now He remains the teacher.

One last time He seeks to draw their attention to the wickedness of men's hearts and the beauty of His love.

Why?

Because it was the wickedness of men's hearts that motivated His steps.

He would glorify the Father by laying His life down for the sheep—sheep that were wicked, sheep that were corrupt—sheep like us.

He would paint a picture of the tenderness of God toward sinners . . .

. . . with His body as the canvas

. . . and His blood as the paint.

Lord Jesus,

these are some of Your last words.

Even in these moments You were teaching.

You comforted those who mourned.

Surely, Your compassion never fails.

Help me to live passionately for and like You.

Help me to live, even to the last moments of my life,

so as to teach others

of the greatness of Your love,

and the beauty of Your holiness.

For Your glory I ask this,

Amen.

Chapter 8

The Savior is stripped and nailed to the cross.

Adapted from the accounts of
Ps 22:16-18; Mt 27:35-37; Mk 15:22; Lk 23:33-35, Jn 19:20

Jesus' humiliation is predicted and accomplished.

FOR DOGS ENCOMPASS ME;
A COMPANY OF EVILDOERS ENCIRCLES ME;
THEY HAVE PIERCED MY HANDS AND FEET—
I CAN COUNT ALL MY BONES—
THEY STARE AND GLOAT OVER ME;
(PSALM 22:16-17)

And they brought Him to the place called Golgotha (which means Place of the Skull). It was there that they crucified Him and the criminals, one on His right and one on His left. And when they had crucified Him, they divided His garments among them by casting lots.

Then they sat down and kept watch over Him. And over His head they put the charge against Him, which Pilate had written. It read,

"This is Jesus, the King of the Jews."

Many of the Jews read this inscription, for the place where Jesus was crucified was near the city, and it was written in Aramaic, Latin, and Greek.

And the people stood by watching, but the rulers, the chief priests, the scribes and elders mocked and scoffed at Him, saying,

"He saved others; let him save himself, if he is the Christ of God, His Chosen One! Let him come down now from the cross, and we will believe in him. He trusts in God; let God deliver him now, if He desires him. For he said 'I am the Son of God.'"

Devotional

A rocky place resembling a skull—that was where they took Him—to murder Him. There they continued their mockery and torture. There they nailed Him to the cross.

On either side of Him hang two known and deserving criminals. Above Him hangs a sign written in three languages,

"Jesus, King of the Jews."

Exactly who He was.

Exactly who He claimed to be.

Exactly why He was crucified.

Even a place known for its resemblance to a skull and its associations with the Roman death machinery of the time couldn't change the fact that He was and is the sovereign Lord of Life, the long-expected Son, the one destined to sit on King David's throne.

The Apostle Paul was mesmerized by the image of our sins being nailed to the cross, canceling out the debt we owed by the atoning sacrifice of the Savior in our place. He penned these words to drive the significance of Christ's sacrifice into the memory of those who believe in Him.

> "And you, who were dead in your trespasses …God made alive together with Him, having forgiven us all our trespasses, by canceling the record of debt that stood against us with its legal demands. This He set aside, nailing it to the cross."
>
> (Colossians 2:13-14)

They echo the prophet Isaiah's words written eight hundred years before Christ: (ISAIAH 53:6)

> "ALL WE LIKE SHEEP HAVE GONE ASTRAY;
> WE HAVE TURNED EVERY ONE TO HIS OWN WAY;
> AND THE LORD HAS LAID ON HIM
> THE INIQUITY OF US ALL."

Crucified Savior,

Your arms were stretched out and

nailed to a tree,

but it was my sin You bore,

my sin that was nailed there with You.

They stole Your clothes,

Your dignity, and Your life,

but not Your love.

You let them nail Your love to the cross.

Help me to understand the depth of Your

passion for me as Your child.

In Your saving name,

Amen.

Chapter 9

The Savior is mocked and soldiers gamble over His clothes.

Adapted from the accounts of
Mt 27:35-44; Mk 15:24-25; Lk 23:34-38;Jn 19:23-25

Crucified between two thieves.

And when they had crucified Him, they divided His garments into four parts among themselves by casting lots. Then they sat down and kept watch over Him. But the tunic was seamless, woven in one piece from top to bottom, so they said to one another,

"Let us not tear it, but cast lots for it to see whose it shall be."

This was to fulfill the Scripture, which says,

"THEY DIVIDED MY GARMENTS AMONG THEM,
AND FOR MY CLOTHING THEY CAST LOTS."
(PS. 22:18)

So the soldiers did these things, and it was the third hour [9 AM] when they crucified Him.

And those who passed by derided Him, wagging their heads and saying,

"You who would destroy the temple and rebuild it in three days, save yourself! If you are the Son of God, come down from the cross."

And the robbers who were crucified with Him also reviled Him in the same way.

And Jesus said,

> *"Father, forgive them, for they know not*
> *what they do."*

And the people stood by, watching, but the rulers scoffed at Him, saying,

"He saved others; let him save himself, if he is the Christ of God, His Chosen One!"

Devotional

He hangs above them now, blood oozing from His back, head, hands, and feet. Below Him, callous-hearted soldiers gamble for His clothing.

It is as if all pity has been drained from the world. The mocking from the crowd continues. The disciples are hiding. Only a few women and the Apostle John are near.

And then, Jesus speaks—He prays for those who mock Him, for those who gamble over His clothing!

> *"Father, forgive them, for they*
> *know not what they do."*

Here is the heart of God revealed: Jesus forgives, even from the cross. His forgiveness is offered to those who have despitefully abused Him. He asks the Father to be merciful to them! O how great is the love and mercy and kindness of God!

Twenty-one centuries later, the resurrected Lord Jesus continues to offer His forgiveness, continues to call men and women to belief in Him and promises that He who conquered death has the power and will to forgive us our sins and give us life eternal.

Forgiving Savior,

Your mercy and grace are food

to a starving soul.

Thank You for the forgiveness

for which I am so undeserving

and yet so desperately need.

I prove each day how much I need Your grace—

Your undeserved favor—by taking Your

forgiveness for granted.

Forgive me and help me to cherish the

extravagance of Your mercy. Make me a

forgiver like You.

For Your glory O Christ,

Amen.

Chapter 10

The Savior is forsaken by the Father.

Adapted from the accounts of
Psalm 22:1-31; Mt 27:45-46; Mk 15:33-34

Jesus applies Psalm 22 to Himself.

Now from the sixth hour [noon] there was darkness over all the land until the ninth hour. And about the ninth hour Jesus cried out with a loud voice, saying,

"*Eloi, Eloi, lema sabachthani?*" that is,

"My God, My God, why have you forsaken Me?"

MY GOD, MY GOD,
WHY HAVE YOU FORSAKEN ME?
WHY ARE YOU SO FAR FROM SAVING ME,
FROM THE WORDS OF MY GROANING?

O MY GOD, I CRY BY DAY,
BUT YOU DO NOT ANSWER,
AND BY NIGHT,
BUT I FIND NO REST.

YET YOU ARE HOLY,
ENTHRONED ON THE PRAISES OF ISRAEL.
IN YOU OUR FATHERS TRUSTED;
THEY TRUSTED, AND YOU DELIVERED THEM.

TO YOU THEY CRIED AND WERE RESCUED;
IN YOU THEY TRUSTED
AND WERE NOT PUT TO SHAME.

BUT I AM A WORM AND NOT A MAN,
SCORNED BY MANKIND
AND DESPISED BY THE PEOPLE.

ALL WHO SEE ME MOCK ME;
THEY MAKE MOUTHS AT ME;
THEY WAG THEIR HEADS; SAYING

"HE TRUSTED ON THE LORD
THAT HE WOULD DELIVER HIM:
LET HIM DELIVER HIM,
SEEING HE DELIGHTED IN HIM."

(PSALM 22:1-8)

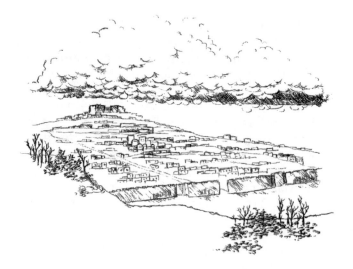

Devotional

It was the ninth hour of the day, 3:00 PM by our reckoning. Hanging in silent agony for some time, He opens His mouth and reveals what His heart has been meditating upon through the six hours of agony on the cross—the twenty-second Psalm.

He applies the psalm to Himself.

All of our words fail.

How do we comprehend the magnitude of this event? God the Son feels forsaken by the Father! How can it be? How is it possible? Finite minds cannot penetrate the mystery of the Infinite One who is Triune, or of separation between the Father and beloved Son, or the vastness of His plan to save those who would believe.

Surely, you too have been forsaken at some point in your life. Yet how can we even begin to comprehend the sense of loss and agony that Christ must have felt?

Infinite relational intimacy with infinite beauty, love, holiness, glory, righteousness, compassion—perfection lost, as the Father turns His back on the sin-bearing Son.

I have been forsaken,

and I wish never to experience it again.

But You went to the cross for me knowing the

price, however temporary, would be

the unimaginable loss of fellowship

with the Father.

I can never repay—

even to try is an insult

to the suffering You endured.

Thank You for the promise that by Your death

heaven's gates have opened wide,

and I too will one day enjoy fellowship

with the Father through You

Jesus Christ, my Lord and Savior.

Amen.

Chapter 11

The Savior tastes bitter wine.

Adapted from the accounts of
Psalm 69; Mt 27:48; Mk 15:35-36; Jn 19:28-30

Jesus thirsts.

And some of the bystanders hearing it said,

"Behold, he is calling Elijah."

After this, Jesus, knowing that all was now finished, said (to fulfill the Scripture),

"I thirst."

And immediately, one of them ran and took a sponge, filled it with sour wine, and put it on a hyssop reed and held it to His mouth to give Him a drink, saying, ...

"Wait, let us see whether Elijah will come to take him down."

REPROACHES HAVE BROKEN MY HEART,
SO THAT I AM IN DESPAIR.
I LOOKED FOR PITY, BUT THERE WAS NONE,
AND FOR COMFORTERS, BUT I FOUND NONE.

THEY GAVE ME POISON FOR FOOD,
AND FOR MY THIRST
THEY GAVE ME SOUR WINE TO DRINK.

(PSALM 69:20-21)

When Jesus had received the sour wine, He said,

"It is finished."

Devotional

Death is not far away now. It is a given that the condemned will die, and the soldiers are more relaxed knowing that there will be no attempt to save the dying men hanging above them. Now the curious bystanders draw closer.

.

And the mocking continues.

When Jesus cries out that He thirsts, someone in the crowd, as a cruel joke but in fulfillment of Scripture, offers Him sour wine.

The cruelty of offering a thirsty and dying man sour wine is hard to imagine. Then again, maybe it isn't.

I remember going to the movie *The Elephant Man.* I was appalled by the cruelty people inflicted upon a fellow human being.

Then a strange thing happened. As I continued to watch I began to feel more and more uncomfortable. I could remember times when I had been similarly cruel, harsh and insensitive myself.

And then I understood the appropriateness of the silence that fell on the theatre as the crowd exited the movie—they had experienced it too—the inescapable feeling of guilt. We had all been stunned into silence by the evil we had seen and saw in ourselves. Was the crowd silent at the Savior's death?

Compassionate and gracious Lord,

my own cruel, harsh comments

and insensitive behavior

leave me no room to feel self-righteous.

I need Your forgiveness like a desert needs rain.

Thank You for the cup You drank on my behalf.

Help me to drink the cup

that You choose for me.

Because Your name is worthy,

Amen.

Chapter 12
The Savior dies on the cross
for our sin.

Adapted from the accounts of
Mt 27:49-56; Mk 15:37-41; Lk 23:44-49

The temple veil is torn in two.

And Jesus cried out again with a loud voice,

"Father, into Your hands
I commit My spirit!"

Having said this, He breathed His last, and yielded up His spirit.

And behold, the curtain of the temple was torn in two, from top to bottom. And the earth shook, and the rocks were split. The tombs also were opened. And many bodies of the saints who had fallen asleep were raised, and coming out of the tombs after His resurrection they went into the holy city and appeared to many.

When the centurion and those who were with Him, keeping watch over Jesus, saw the earthquake and what took place, they were filled with awe and said,

"Truly this was the Son of God!"

And the centurion praised God, saying,

"Certainly this man was innocent!"

And the crowds assembled for this spectacle, when they saw what had taken place, returned home beating their breasts.

There were also many women there, looking on from a distance, who had followed Jesus from Galilee, ministering to Him, among whom were Mary Magdalene and Mary the mother of James the younger and of Joses, and Salome, and Joseph and the mother of the sons of Zebedee. And there were also many other women who came up with Him to Jerusalem.

Devotional

Isaac Watts poured out in song the appropriate response of the believing heart to the cross of Christ.

> When I survey the wondrous cross,
> On which the Prince of Glory died,
> My richest gain I count but loss,
> And pour contempt on all my pride.
>
> Forbid it, Lord, that I should boast,
> Save in the death of Christ, my God;
> All the vain things that charm me most,
> I sacrifice them to His blood.
>
> See, from His head, His hands, His feet
> Sorrow and love flow mingled down,
> Did e'er such love and sorrow meet,
> Or thorns compose so rich a crown?
>
> Were the whole realm of nature mine,
> That were a present far too small;
> Love so amazing, so divine,
> Demands my soul, my life, my all.

> When I Survey the Wondrous Cross
> Text by: Isaac Watts (1674-1748)

Prince of Glory,

Lord of Life,

Your love is so stunning in its perfection.

Help me to daily preach the cross to my soul.

Help me to live always in the shadow of

Your sacrifice for me.

Help me to give my soul, my life, my all

in loving and faithful service to You.

Lord of Life, be my life.

For the spread of Your fame,

Amen.

Chapter 13

The Savior's side is pierced by a spear.

Adapted from the accounts of
Exodus 12:46; Numbers 9:12 and John 19:31-37

Jesus is pierced in fulfillment of Scripture.

[The Passover had been celebrated for over 1,400 years.
The fire of its rituals and patterns and associations had been
burned into the Jewish soul. Every Jewish family knew that
care must be taken to not break the bones of the sacrificial
lamb. Passages like the following had been memorized and
could be recited by heart.]

IT (the Passover lamb) SHALL BE EATEN IN ONE
HOUSE; YOU SHALL NOT TAKE ANY OF THE FLESH
OUTSIDE THE HOUSE, AND YOU SHALL NOT
BREAK ANY OF ITS BONES.
Exodus 12:46

THEY SHALL LEAVE NONE OF IT UNTIL THE
MORNING, NOR BREAK ANY OF ITS BONES;
ACCORDING TO ALL THE STATUTE FOR THE
PASSOVER THEY SHALL KEEP IT.
Numbers 9:12

Since it was the day of Preparation, and so that the bodies would not remain on the cross on the Sabbath (for that Sabbath was a high day), the Jews asked Pilate that their legs might be broken and that they might be taken away.

So the soldiers came and broke the legs of the first and of the other who had been crucified with Him. But when they came to Jesus and saw that He was already dead, they did not break His legs. But one of the soldiers pierced His side with a spear, and at once there came out blood and water.

He who saw it has borne witness—his testimony is true, and he knows that he is telling the truth—in order that you also may believe.

For these things took place that the Scripture might be fulfilled:

"NOT ONE OF HIS BONES WILL BE BROKEN."

And again another Scripture says,

"THEY WILL LOOK ON HIM
WHOM THEY HAVE PIERCED."

Devotional

The soldiers mutilate the body, and God brings to fulfillment the Scripture: (ZECHARIAH 12:10)

> "AND I WILL POUR OUT ON THE HOUSE OF DAVID AND THE INHABITANTS OF JERUSALEM A SPIRIT OF GRACE AND PLEAS FOR MERCY, SO THAT, WHEN THEY LOOK ON ME, ON HIM WHOM THEY HAVE PIERCED, THEY SHALL MOURN FOR HIM, AS ONE MOURNS FOR AN ONLY CHILD, AND WEEP BITTERLY OVER HIM, AS ONE WEEPS OVER A FIRSTBORN."

Imagine the heartbreak of the disciples and of the courageous women who, along with the apostle John, did not run and hide. The disciples have not only the loss of Jesus and the brutality of His death, but the dashed hopes of their own dreams and the memories of their own cowardice with which to contend.

The women and John have seen up close the tortured body, the agony of both His body and soul, and the piercing of His side that seems to them the final indignity.

Emotions and memory collide from so many different directions that they feel like petrified wood— cold, lifeless and hard.

They are numb in their exhaustion, aimless in their confusion, broken by their sorrow. Where do they go? What can they do?

What is there left to do but weep?

Zechariah's words perfectly match the cry of their hearts.

> THEY SHALL MOURN FOR HIM, AS ONE
> MOURNS FOR AN ONLY CHILD, AND WEEP
> BITTERLY OVER HIM, AS ONE WEEPS OVER A
> FIRSTBORN."

Pierced but triumphant Lord,

Your body was pierced through for our transgressions.

You were crushed for our iniquities.

You bore the iniquity of us all

and purchased with Your own blood

our redemption.

Truly, truly You are the Way, the Truth,

and the Life.

Help me never to forget the spectacular

and lavish display of Your love.

Help me fix my gaze

upon the beauty of Your holiness

and never let me wander from Your commandments.

In Your holy name,

Amen

Chapter 14

The Savior's body is taken down and entombed.

Adapted from the accounts of Mt 27:57-66; Mk 15:42-47
Lk 23:50-56; Jn 19:38-42

Jesus is sealed in the tomb.

When it was evening on the day of Preparation, that is, the day before the Sabbath, there came a rich man from Arimathea named Joseph, a respected member of the Council, a good and righteous man, who also was a disciple of Jesus. He had not consented to their decision and action and was looking for the kingdom of God. Though he feared the Jews, he took courage and went to Pilate and asked for the body of Jesus secretly.

Pilate was surprised to hear that He had already died. Summoning the centurion, he asked him whether Jesus was already dead. And when he learned from the centurion that He was, he granted the corpse to Joseph.

Nicodemus also, who earlier had come to Jesus by night, came bringing a mixture of myrrh and aloes, about seventy-five pounds in weight. So they took the body of Jesus and bound it in linen cloths with the spices, as is the burial custom of the Jews. Then they laid the body in Joseph's own new tomb, which he had cut in the rock.

No one had ever yet been laid in the tomb. And they rolled a great stone to the entrance and went away.

Mary Magdalene and the other Mary were there, siting opposite the tomb, and saw where and how the body was laid.

So they returned and prepared spices and ointments. On the Sabbath they rested according to the commandment. The next day, that is, after the day of Preparation, the chief priests and the Pharisees gathered before Pilate and said,

"Sir, we remember how that impostor said, while he was still alive, 'After three days I will rise.'

"Therefore order the tomb to be made secure until the third day, lest his disciples go and steal him away and tell the people, 'He has risen from the dead,' and the last fraud will be worse than the first."

Pilate said to them,

"You have a guard of soldiers. Go, make it as secure as you can."

So they went and made the tomb secure by sealing the stone and setting a guard.

Devotional

Every picture, every painting of Christ being taken down from the cross is designed to convey a deep sadness and loss, layers of sorrow that words somehow seem inadequate to fully express. So the artists try to use paint and canvas rather than words and parchment, and still they fall short of the heartbreaking reality of the Lamb of God's death.

Limp and lifeless, He is taken down. He is laid in a tomb, in fulfillment of Scripture—the tomb of a rich man. Isaiah prophesied it 800 years before with these words: (ISAIAH 53:9)

> HIS GRAVE WAS ASSIGNED WITH WICKED MEN,
> YET HE WAS WITH A RICH MAN IN HIS DEATH,
> BECAUSE HE HAD DONE NO VIOLENCE,
> NOR WAS THERE ANY DECEIT IN HIS MOUTH.

Of course He had done no violence. Of course there was no deceit in His mouth. He was the spotless, sinless Passover Lamb. He was the One to whom John the Baptist pointed and declared:

"Behold the Lamb of God,
Who takes away the sins of the world."
(John 1:29)

But we have sinned.

We have lost our tempers. We have called people fools. We have lied. We have stolen. We have used the

Lord's name in vain. We have dishonored our parents. We have broken every one of the Ten Commandments in our hearts. In other words, we are—all of us—lying, thieving, dishonoring, and blaspheming sinners standing guilty before a holy God. Violence and deceit have been with us all our lives ... but not in Him.

He was perfect. And now He is laid in a tomb. It is Good Friday and the whole world is shrouded in darkness.

Spotless Lamb of God,

You lay dead in Joseph's tomb,

so that I could walk in newness of life.

Without Your death, I would have no hope.

Because You died,

I have heaven.

Thank You for the cross.

Help me to understand the significance of the cross

and to lift it high so that others

would be drawn to You and the mercy that You give.

For the glory of God, I pray.

Amen.

A Final Challenge

Christ died. But He rose again on the third day, just as He had promised He would. And the world has never been the same.

Christians down through the ages have summarized His life and teachings so that others could come to know and love Him as they do.

In the early second century, perhaps as early as A.D. 130, an anonymous disciple penned these words:

> "When our wickedness had reached its height, and it had been clearly shown that its reward—punishment and death—was impending over us .... God Himself took on Him the burden of our iniquities. He gave His own Son as a ransom for us, the holy One for transgressors, the blameless One for the wicked, the righteous One for the

unrighteous, the incorruptible One for the corruptible, the immortal One for them that are mortal.

For what other thing was capable of covering our sins than His righteousness? By what other one was it possible that we, the wicked and ungodly, could be justified, than by the only Son of God?

O sweet exchange! O unsearchable operation! O benefits surpassing all expectation! That the wickedness of many should be hid in a single righteous One, and that the righteousness of One should justify many transgressors!"

There is great beauty in this early Christian's words. You can sense both his passion for Christ and the humility of his own heart as he writes about the great exchange of our wickedness for the righteousness of Christ.

Have you trusted in the Christ? Do you know Him as your personal sin-bearer? Right now, in the quietness of your own soul you can receive Him and His gifts of forgiveness and eternal life. If you would like to do that, I want to encourage you to talk directly to Christ. Perhaps the prayer on the next page will capture your own thoughts and confession to God.

"Lord Jesus, I need You. Thank You for dying on the cross for my sins. I can never earn or hope to repay what You have done for me. I open the door of my life and receive You as my Savior and Lord. Thank You for forgiving my sins and giving me eternal life. Take my life and make me the kind of person You want me to be. I love You. Help me to learn how to love You better. Amen.

If you trusted in Christ today, and have expressed it with that prayer, tell someone. Please take a moment and write us at the following address:

New Song Church
151 E. Briarcliff Road.
Bolingbrook, IL 60440

Or you can e-mail us at

Info@NewSong-Church.com

We would be honored to help you begin your own adventure with Christ.

"It's

Friday,

but

Sunday's

coming."

The Sojourning Press
Exploring a cross-shaped life

"For you are but aliens and sojourners with Me."
Leviticus 25:23b (ESV)

The Sojourning Press exists to help believers adopt the lifestyle of a sojourner and live passionately for and like Christ. We believe that that we are a "cross-bought and cross-shaped people." We strive to produce books, papers, articles and events that stir a passionate devotion for the Master of our souls and help the body of Christ toward a radical rediscovery of intimacy with the Savior.

For information on resources and materials contact us at the address listed below:

The Sojourning Press

151 E. Briarcliff Road
Bolingbrook, Illinois 60440

Beloved, I urge you as sojourners and
exiles to abstain from the passions of the
flesh, which wage war against your soul.
1 Peter 2:11 (ESV)

About the Author:

Marty Schoenleber, Jr. is a church planter, teaching pastor and published poet. He has taught at three different seminaries but his favorite title is "Dad." Marty loves Jesus, his wife, his children, church planting, books, books, baseball, Philadelphia Eagles football, the music of U2 and Caedmon's Call, Philly cheese steaks, and more books.

Beyond Jesus, his heroes are his Dad, (who lives with Jesus now), his mom (who lives in Pennsylvania), C.S. Lewis, John Piper, Walker Percy and Stephen R. Donaldson. Marty has had one book published by Broadman/Holman Publishers, but the title is too long to remember. Fortunately, Amazon.com remembers it for him. *Experience the Passion of Christ* is his second book for The Sojourning Press.

About the Artist:

Carol Gundersen is the token Canadian in the office at New Song Church. She works as the communications assistant, which means we consult with her on all things artistic. She is a mother of two talented daughters and the wife of one talented husband. Carol attended Moody Bible Institute, which also happens to be where she met her talented husband. If you ever visit New Song Church you can see some of her artwork and talent on display in the Bolingbrook Christian Health Clinic where one of her murals adorns the wall and delights the patients. Carol loves to read, is an unbelievable cook, and enjoys spending time in her new studio at home. Her favorite authors are C. S. Lewis and Farley Mowat.